Little Dog's BIG Adventure

by Melinda Maycock

PublishAmerica
Baltimore

First printing

ISBN1-59286-873-8
PUBLISHED BY PUBLISHAMERICA, LLLP
www.publishamerica.com
Baltimore

Printed in the United States of America

For my children

Little Dog lived in the country. He would sit under the oak tree and dream of going to the BIG city and the adventures he would have.

Little Dog would always tell his mother about his adventures and would ask when he really could go. “Someday,” his mother would reply.

One day, his mother let him go to the BIG city.

They hopped on her little motorcycle and she drove him there.

When Little Dog got to the BIG city, he saw tall buildings and…a BIG train.

“I must ride on that BIG train,” said Little Dog. He boarded the BIG train.

The train rode on the rail. It rode and rode…all the way back to the country!

“I don’t want to be in the country,” Little Dog cried to his mother. “I want to be in the BIG city.” Little Dog’s mother brought him back to the BIG city.

He saw tall buildings, lots of people and…a BIG helicopter.

“I must fly in that BIG helicopter,” said Little Dog.
He sat in the BIG helicopter.

The helicopter flew high in the air. It flew and flew…all the way back to the country!

“I don’t want to be in the country,” Little Dog cried to his mother. “I want to be in the BIG city.” Little Dog’s mother brought him back to the BIG city.

He saw tall buildings, lots of people, colorful balloons and…a BIG bus.

“I must ride on that BIG bus,” said Little Dog. He stepped onto the BIG bus.

The bus drove on the road. It drove and drove…all the way back to the country!

"I don't want to be in the country," Little Dog cried to his mother. "I want to be in the BIG city." Little Dog's mother brought him back to the BIG city.

I am not going to ride on anything else, Little Dog told himself. He walked around the BIG city and saw many new things.

It started to get late. Little Dog was getting tired. He missed his mother. He wanted to go home. *I know,* thought Little Dog, *I will go see the BIG bus, and ask him to take me home.*

“I am sorry,” said the BIG bus to Little Dog. “I have a flat tire and it will not be fixed until morning.

Go see the helicopter."
Little Dog went to see the BIG helicopter.

“Will you take me home?” Little Dog asked. “I am sorry,” said the BIG helicopter. “My rotor is broken and I cannot fly.

Maybe the train can help you." Little Dog went to see the BIG train.

“I am sorry. I cannot take you home,” said the BIG train to Little Dog. “My driver has gone home for the night.”

Little Dog put his head down and started to cry. *How am I going to get home now?* he wondered. Little Dog heard a beep. He looked up.

It was his mother! He hopped on her little motorcycle. The motorcycle rode through the city streets.

It rode and rode…all the way back to the country!